GUILTY
BY
ASSOCIATION

The fear of stagnation
Is motivation to stay
Strong willed despite
Peer confrontation

N Shawayne   Jan 12 2017
(Thank you for the support
Annessa)

GUILTY BY ASSOCIATION

Shawayne Dunstan

Copyright © 2016 by Shawayne Dunstan.

ISBN: Softcover   978-1-5245-5109-4
             eBook   978-1-5245-5108-7

All rights reserved. No part of this book may be reproduced or transmitted in any form or by any means, electronic or mechanical, including photocopying, recording, or by any information storage and retrieval system, without permission in writing from the copyright owner.

Any people depicted in stock imagery provided by Thinkstock are models, and such images are being used for illustrative purposes only.
Certain stock imagery © Thinkstock.

Print information available on the last page.

Rev. date: 10/11/2016

To order additional copies of this book, contact:
Xlibris
1-888-795-4274
www.Xlibris.com
Orders@Xlibris.com
751550

Contents

Descendant 1
Passion 2
The Beauty in the Struggle 3
A Mind such as Mine 4
Monsters of the Night 5
Innocence is not heard of.. 6
Throughout Life 7
Identity of a Stranger 8
Some Nights 9
Someone to hold 10
Solace 11
Overdose 12
Cleansed 13
Cheers 14
Dreams 15
Sunset 16
The Woman in Black 17
Goal 18
The Lady in Red 19
Liar 20
Lucy 21
Anti-Depressant 22
Cowardice 23
I've got you 24
Chances are… 25
Do Not Mourn Me 26
The Rose 27
How Convenient 28
Monique 29
The Poet 30
Clash 31

My Regards 32
Spark 33
Nathalie 34
Deceitful Heart 35
Opposites Attract 36
Peace of Mind 37
Purple 38
The Cost of a Dime 39
What Remains 41
To My Unborn Child 42
Potential 43
Fin 44

Dedicated to all those curious

Descendant

I heard voices
When I was a child
They sung and screamed
These words to me
That I have somehow forged
Into the poetry that you see.

Passion

A thousand seconds
Condemned to silence as they tick away
No words are required
For actions portray our burning passions
For one another
The intoxicating heat that ignites from inside
Shared by two lovers
Isolated from peering eyes
Engulfed by darkness
Not a moment too soon
Passionate affection
Witnessed only by the moon.

The Beauty in the Struggle

I have the tendency to drink Hennessey
With frenemies who don't want to see me achieve
"There's beauty in the struggle
And we don't want you to leave…"
Unfortunately that means a life of poverty and regret
I haven't eaten in a week
Yet I'm still in debt
I refuse to remain stagnant
Along with all the others who've become Institutionalized
How to get a better life
Is what I've recently prioritized
Either I can sit back and watch as everything passes me by
In this fast moving life
Or I can think twice when they hand me the Ultimatum
For a "suitable" price…

A Mind such as Mine

Enter a mind such as mine
And see what you find
In the meantime I'll procrastinate
While you salivate
Over dreams that you'll never achieve
I tiptoe on tightropes over open volcanoes
With my eyes closed constantly
At night I don't sleep
Instead I listen out for these compelling voices
That keep calling out to me

Your eyes are bleeding with envy
It's easy to see that you clearly resent me
My pockets are completely empty
Mortal men have been competing for centuries.

Monsters of the Night

Uncontrollable cravings
Sweet temptations
Soothing rhythm
History in the making

Acid rain pours
Steel locks on broken doors
Hallow embraces from skeletons
Emotions that are irrelevant

Unknown forces bind me
In between dreams and reality
Lungs filled with toxic smoke
Ignited by a lighter
As I attempted to cope

Coldest winds welcomed me home
Flashing lights, but I've lost my phone
Deception hidden in plain sight
Monsters arise on this moonlit night

Innocence is not heard of....

Rusted chains along with a mind and hands aching to break free

To glimpse freedom before it is taken away forever

Only to soon become a figment of my unholy imagination

A crime not committed
But still I must be submitted
Against my will to close a case
And inside I feel the rage
Rising and descending
As if it were a lost tidal wave
Wrong place, wrong time, and wrong crime
Why must everything be wrong
Is there no innocence in this web of lies
Entangled with anger, temptation and deception?

My memory is weak along with my weary body
I want to cry, but the tears have dried up out of my eyes
But through my sorrows I see myself...the true me
Not the life that I have lived
So many questions to be asked
But the most important is here at last

Who am I?

Throughout Life

Nourish the mind with knowledge
Purify the soul with justice
Satisfy the heart with love
And give gratitude for everything sent from above.

Identity of a Stranger

Who am I?!
I ask myself screaming into the mirror
The face, the eyes, cheek and chin
None of its mine, it's all a lie
A personality portrayed from deep within
To mask the pain and all my sins.

Some Nights

Some nights I close my eyes
And my childhood goes up in smoke

Darkened clouds
Suffocating fumes
Blinding fog
Figures I drew

I witnessed my mother weeping and badly bruised tucked in a corner of a home I thought I knew. I see the smoldering outline of my father, his back to the burning building we used to call a house.

The front lawn is scattered with matches...

Someone to hold

We both know that its murder she wrote
On crumbled suicide notes
Just before she grabbed that rope
And wrapped it around her throat
Because she couldn't cope
Some stuff can't be numbed with dope
Or morphine
Yet we still indulge in them to escape realty
Weary bodies whispering R.I.P
Within gloomy cemeteries
Located where the sun don't shine
And it rains all the time
Salty tears flow, but we say we're fine
At night we think about memories and false serenities
As we drink wine
Its murder she wrote
To the tune of hollow piano notes
A decision which she chose
Even though we didn't want her to go.

Solace

Turquoise sheets
Noisy alarm
Creaking floors
Lucky charms

Morning news
Residue of dew
Birds chirping
While gazing at you

Strawberry lips
Blueberry mist
Unbearable temptation
Hands on your hips

Moon is a witness to what we do
Late nights spent comforting you
Swiftly out the door I head once more
This time without uttering your name
Because I know in times of desperation
You will call upon me again…

Overdose

Imagine how it feels
When your throat closes up
And your eyes start to bleed
As the speakers continue playing
Bohemian Rhapsody

Imagine how it feels
When a better liquid
Soaks up your sleeve
And your eyes become blurry
As you struggle to walk steadily

Imagine how it feels
Waking up in the middle of nowhere
With mysterious scars all over your body
And different shades of dye in your hair

Imagine how it feels
Watching lights race by above you
As you're rushed to a unfamiliar room
With unfamiliar faces
Who run numerous tests

Imagine how it feels…but you can't
Because you just overdosed
Infront of individuals who you though cared about you the most.

Cleansed

Last night I went to sleep with shackles on my feet
All because I'm highly influenced by the friends I keep
Last night I was a victim of a horrific scene
Extended barrels and sharpened daggers pointed at me
Reality struck when my cousin caught a bullet and shook
Immediately I questioned the value of everything we took
Vengeance motivated us to return to that block
A drive by took place leaving behind a dozen shots
Today I jumped up from haunting dreams
Armed with the mentality that nothing is what it seems
Today I sat back rather than intervene
Who was I to demand peace when my own hands weren't clean
There will come a day when your heart turns cold
A winner will be crowned between the forces who fight for your soul
No longer will you be fazed by gold
But you will test the authenticity of everything you're told
The sky is black; leaving you shrouded in darkness
You walk on tightropes strung over the abyss
Words are potent, but that's not important
You may be holy, but the devil wants 50%
Throwing up confessions as you drown in cement
Lungs cry out for air, but you need to be cleansed.

Cheers

Cheers to every bullet that missed
Shaking fingers hugging triggers
Aimed at adrenaline filled hearts
Cheers to running shoes
With fading soles
Which despite their appearance
Still carried me away
Cheers to all the days
As I continue to survive them
Sunrise to sunset
Cursed is the day
A bulletproof vest
Becomes my best friend.

Dreams

Demons haunt me in these horror-filled dreams
Venturing through dark valleys while sanity is nowhere to be seen
Looking for a sign because all I truly desire is freedom of mind
Crooked eyes watch in silence as I fall to my demise
Chilling winds rattle my bones
Eerie melodies are all that I hear
All I really want is to go home
But then suddenly the menacing creature reappears
It is not an animal nor a man
Midnight fur, booming voice and glistening fangs
The earth shakes when it steps, coming closer for I am next
I smell its last victim on its breath and within that moment I feel totally helpless
I try to run, but I cannot breathe, it chases me with the intent to feed
Demons haunt me in these horror filled dreams
Have you not heard the blood-curdling screams?

Sunset

A metallic taste lies upon my tongue
Shadows seem to hover all around
My thirst has been quenched, but hunger still lives inside
There is something lurking within my eyes
The frozen ground leaves evidence of my presence
Darkened clouds and winds that are simply restless
I've lost my coat and my hands have scars
Sounds of sirens are still so far
I take refuge underneath a willow tree
One with a thick trunk and colorful leaves
Creeping over a mountain, how brightly the sun shone
In a matter of seconds all that was left was ash and bones.

The Woman in Black

Through her window a million doves
Are perched silently upon a willow tree
Rain continues to pour down endlessly
As grey clouds weep
The tears from her eyes crystallized
Against her skin
The house was quiet except for the tapping
Which came from deep within
Rusted pipes run dry
While white sheets remain tangled
Muddy footprints all over the tile floor
The lock on the front door is mangled
A woman sits patiently by the window
In a dress with ripped sleeves
Fog crept underneath the door
But she did not stir
Instead she began to mourn
All those who had abandoned her
A brownstone home
Remains undisturbed down the street
On stormy nights
A shadow sits by the window and weeps.

Goal

While many others around me
Keep chasing desires endlessly
I occupy myself with the person
Who makes me feel so free
Features of this individual not only intrigues
But their warm hands reassure in times my body
Is attacked by the cold breeze
And when my innocent heart bleeds
This person sings beautiful melodies to me
As we laid beneath numerous oak tress
A world of our own created by us
A world of our own that was suitably enough
The sun may sleep, but the moon will rise
No better sight than waking up and seeing those blue eyes
I am not fazed by fame or gold
My only goal is acquiring someone to hold
Many others around me
Keep chasing desires endlessly
But his is not new
My only intention was making someone happy
And that person is you.

The Lady in Red

She smokes me slower
Than cigarettes
After she has reached ecstasy
She hungrily feasts on my body
Like a foreign delicacy
Eyes that seem to bleed
Captivate me so much
That I am paralyzed
We play a dangerous game
With ice and fire
Opposites attract despite what you say
On afternoons I hear her talking to the moon
Speaking of furious storms that would come soon
This woman in red with strands down her back
Thick lips sent vibrations whenever they smacked
She is a warrior in disguise
A ruthless killer who is not shy
She sits on her throne playing with knives
Expert aim that has ended lives
Steel blades stick out from my back
Uncontrollable anger that caused her to attack
Do not be fooled for this is not love
Because to her I was replaceable
Like taking off a glove.

Liar

Oh darling don't you ever trust me
I am a liar can you not see?
The smile is tainted and my mind has been born anew
All my intentions are filled with ways of using you
I have no stability nor morality
How is it that you dare to trust me?
Maybe you are unaware of my true identity
Maybe you are unaware of who I become in the night
Funny how such deception can be hidden in plain sight.

Lucy

Lucy been following me
Whispering within these dreams
Lucy been calling on me
Saying that nothing is what it seems
She has me in her grip
And I can't escape
Surely this is a way to go
If I were to die today
Tempting me with lies
Tempting me with fame
Enemies approach with friendly names
While Alley continues to calls me a disgrace

I can't look in my son's eyes
Shivers run down my spine
A snake lingers in the grass
Sharpened venomous fangs
Aimed at me before I could dash
Lucy been following me
Trying to make me happy
Woman, joy and lots of gold

"All you desire in return for your soul."

Anti-Depressant

I am not your Antidepressant...

Even though your parents warned you about me, you still craved the scent of me and my lullabies of peace. Ignited with a flick of a lighter and the puff of your lungs, you escaped reality for the hours to come. You may not see how I see until it is far too late, so I shall stand back, watch and wait. For you are no more than another one of my victims who shall desperately crawl back to me once their "high" is gone.

I am not your Antidepressant

My bitter taste will make you forget about your worries for a few hours. You'll regret in the morning, but require me by two. The world seems to be collapsing and I am the only serenity, so you need me in morning, lunchtime and when you sleep.

I am not your Antidepressant

My words of comfort in these times are all, but gone, there seems to be no medication to help you go on. I sense your craving has consumed you entirely, but I still wait for the day that you no longer need me.

Cowardice

Cowardice is found in me
Whenever our eyes meet
It is during these moments
I "forget" how to speak
Hearts bleed
And souls seem to plead
The result of such avoidance
Is a body filled with grief.

I've got you

My world might be falling apart
But I've always held a special spot for you
In my heart
Past relations have left their mark
But upon this complicated road we shall embark
If there be pain
I shall shelter you once again
If there be loneliness
I shall comfort you
As you shake in that yellow sundress
I shall do for you
What you've done for me
And that is being there
When I truly needed
Company.

Chances are...

Political digression
Has gotten me anxious
During doctor sessions
Because I'm worried about current events
Such as people squeezing triggers
In the name of revenge
If I hold my tongue despite what I see
Then I'll probably be crucified
And thrown into seas of agony
But even if I were to dispute
The powers that control
I'd probably be killed at the feet
Of my three year old.

Do Not Mourn Me

When my breath has ceased
My body pale
Joints still
And pronounced deceased
I beg you
Do not cry
Or mourn for me
Dry your eyes
For shame the misery
Death has been patient
Now he has come for me
We shall meet in the future
Soon I hope
But that is an answer
Only God knows.

The Rose

Settle down for a minute or so
Beneath skeletal trees of this undergrowth
Allow the autumn chill to travel
Down your throat
While our innocent souls make angels
In the undisturbed snow
As cold winds blow
Remind me of all the apologies I owe
I've heard death's raven's crow
But I'd never want to go
With all these regrets in tow
I'm more confident with the less they know
Because as I've always said before
One's true potential in society today
Is equivalent to the rose
That secretly grows
A little more
Everyday.

How Convenient

It wasn't your lips
That I was kissing
I'm sorry
But you're mistaken
The whole night
She was on my mind
And luckily
You were a convenient
Asset at the time...

Monique

Your name is like a foreign delicacy in my mouth
I chew on it slowly before I spit it out
If looks could kill I'd be buried 6ft below
In an isolated lot covered by snow
Your teeth are dripping with greed
My skin still bares scars from when you use to feed on me
False comfort from skeletal trees
So you now dwell in shallow lakes
You're nothing more than a disgrace
If your day came I wouldn't resuscitate
I'd happily dispose of you without a trace
And it wouldn't even be for the scar you left on my face
Your horrible actions can't be erased!
Curse the day I forget my flaws
Curse the day I fall into your grip once more
Evil lurks upon a dark night such as this
Merciless creatures willing to kill a succubus
My fangs drip with the blood of the innocent
My claws have dug quite deep
There used to be a time where no one could stand against me
Until that dreadful day that I met Monique.

The Poet

My eyes are weary
For I am deprived of sleep
The clock is ticking
And I can barely breathe
Pen flowing
As I reach into the depths of my mind
Seeking for something worthy to find
Tracing the paper with memories and sins
Tracing the paper with places I've been
I've been searching for peace
But I know it will never be
Ink stains covered my hands
As I began to weep.

Clash

Darling
You are happiness
In the summertime
Sun shining
Through empty homes
Look beneath
And you'll find
Eulogies carved
Into my bones
Rosy lips
Bring eternal bliss
In seas of agony
I'm a pacifist
So why is it
That you are mad me?

My Regards

I hope everything you love goes up in smoke
And when the cold wind blows
There's no one to help you cope
I hope that you're always given pay cuts
And when your tears fall
You permanently stain your shirt with makeup
I hope you vomit every time you eat
Onto all those tangled sheets
I hope you always lose your key
And you're late for work
Whenever you down a pill
It gets stuck in your throat and hurts
I hope you're never happy again
Abandoned in the falling rain
By all of your friends
Then your teeth fall out
So you can't tell no lies
And you drown in regret
Whenever you sleep with those guys
I hope you get everything you deserve
Including water to quench your everlasting thirst.

Spark

It's amazing isn't it?
How we've grown so close
During both our predicaments
It's quite magnificent
The force that exists
Between you and I
Despite the countless disputes
We've continued to "try"
We both lie
Whenever that happens I can't look you in the eye
While you put up walls
I destroy the ones that weren't fortified
How long will it take
Until one of our hearts permanently breaks?
When everything is smooth we don't appreciate
But when we're apart it seems something is missing
I refuse to say that I love you
Because those words have been far too abused
Doors slam and insults are thrown
I shout, "I want answers!"
While you scream, "I don't like your tone!"
It's amazing how much fury lives within our hearts
It often makes us forget about our special spark.

Nathalie

Confess your love to me
Upon your knees
In fields of vulnerability
As the stars rain down endlessly
Show me eyes that are no longer
Green with envy
Show me lips that have been cleansed of poison
And now drip with honey
If love makes men blind
Then I've stumbled into dark rooms
Numerous times in search of ecstasy
Confess your love to me
In this kitchen
With grey walls that hold us captive
Like a prison
I shall listen
As lies roll beautifully off your tongue
One by one
I shall listen
Even when your words hit me harder
Than the bullets from a loaded gun.

Deceitful Heart

Curse you heart
And your terrible ways
A selfish thing you are
Bringing about pain
You break apart everything
You hold no loyalty
Shattering vows and promises
Chasing desires recklessly
You are fragile to temptations
And intriguing glances
Secrecy is introduced
The night increases chances
Why must you be so unfaithful?
Not only to women, but yourself too
Have you ever stop to wonder
About the things you do?
Lying to your emotions
Leaving her on the floor crying
What is it that you crave?
On the inside, are you dying?
Set out on its latest mark
Unapologetic from the start
Whoever encounters it
Don't trust this deceiving heart!

Opposites Attract

Shall we make love over the corpse
Of your unworthy past lovers
Whilst the clouds in the skies
Shed tears from the eyes of angels
If it is passion flowing through our veins
I would bravely scale tall mountains
And battle foul beasts in order to be with you again
Shower me with your grace
And tell me of your pain
The night is full of evil
Yet I still found serenity within your embrace
This bond has been broken before
Unforgiveable actions as we went out seeking more
Many beautiful figures may have crossed my eyes
But their true intentions were to live lavish lives
In your case many men approached with banknotes
Dimly lit hotel rooms was where you were found the most
Secrets always seem to tear us apart
Hidden within near our hearts
Words are said in anger, but the love is still there
What we have in common is that we both care.

Peace of Mind

The anger which runs through
Is toxic to your veins
Abandon it at once
And do not listen
To these hate-filled whispers
Urging for you to partake

Count down slowly
Walk away
Take the higher ground
Make this your day

Calm the nerves
Settle the mind
Steady the breathing
Open your eyes

No need for harmful interactions
No need for fighting of the factions
Within this moment you were greatly tested
Wise conscience has led to you being peacefully rested.

Purple

I am purple
Carefree, but always prepared
Words are my weapons
Dramatic tactics I bare
I am simple, but blissful
Miracles are essential
Perfection is mandatory.

The Cost of a Dime

Attempting to conquer
Homelessness on the street?
Yesterday I spotted my uncle
Begging for something to eat
About a week later
Crows in sky
Screamed out R.I.P
Dirty hands and damp coat
In this lifestyle of poverty

Never blinked an eye
Or spared a dime
The cost of a dollar is way too high
So I'm going to hold onto this check
Like it's forever mine
"Gluttony at its finest"
I was told a hundred times
Been to the places
Where the sun don't shine
So I'm going to cruise through this life
While sipping fine wine

Stepped out that store
And saw a man on the floor
He jumped up
And began asking for more
Like it was my fault
He was sleeping in a puddle
Rodent infested corner
That he was huddled.

Bloodshot eyes bored into mine
Cracker laced weed rested in his pipe
With bruised fingers
He begged for a dime
With no hesitation I told him
Every one was mine

He asked me if I read the Bible
I told him I had no idols
He said God knows all about me
Then he quoted a verse from
Ecclesiastes

"Whoever loves money never has enough"
"Whoever has money is never satisfied with their income"

What was this supposed to me?
Homeless man quoting scriptures
To satisfy his plea?
Feelings of resentment
Developing inside
Didn't have to look up
To know I was being watched by bloodshot eyes.

What Remains

This tree of life
Was home to googly-eyed children
Who laughed in the face of death
Adrenaline fueled bodies
That cowered underneath fruitless leaves
With snuffed out dreams to succeed
A life of modesty is built to intrigue
But what if you already lack all abilities?
If this is correct then the victim is me
And even though I don't fear death
My downfall is inevitable
Because my confidence is locked away with lock and key
I'm pleading on my knees
While cold sweat and salty tears
Trickle down my face simultaneously
Trust is proven to be dangerous
Yet we still get high on love like angel dust
Raging emotions can be conveyed with a simple touch
Cold hearts melt when they see her blush
I'm not optimistic, I'm pessimistic
A googly-eyed child swimming in a pool of his own secrets.

To My Unborn Child

My child is waiting for me
Ever so anxiously
Waiting to be loved by the affection
Of you and me
Whether in my dreams
Or in reality
Whether in wealth
Or in poverty
I shall boldly take a stand
And protect this child
Rising to the occasion
When they need a helping hand.

Potential

Do not be deceived
By looks from sore eyes
Because even the caterpillar
Can morph into a beautiful butterfly.

Fin

Bloodshot eyes stood over me
As I began questioning my dignity
I've always tried to weave out
The identities of frenemies
Because someone once told me
That sinister smiles lurked beneath
Don't ever make promises you can't keep
Because regret is a puddle that's knee deep
I'm constantly stuck in between dreams and fantasies
Maybe it's because I've always wanted to escape reality.

CPSIA information can be obtained
at www.ICGtesting.com
Printed in the USA
LVOW07s2056271216
518887LV00001B/14/P